D1265977

Guess What

Published in the United States of America by
Cherry Lake Publishing
Ann Arbor, Michigan
www.cherrylakepublishing.com

Content Adviser: Susan Heinrichs Gray
Reading Adviser: Marla Conn, ReadAbility, Inc.
Book Design: Felicia Macheske

Photo Credits: © Eric Isselée/Shutterstock.com, cover, 3, 7, 11, 17, 21, back cover; © Roberto Tetsuo Okamura/
Shutterstock.com, 1, 4; © fotostokers/Shutterstock.com, 8; © Andre Mueller/Shutterstock.com, 12; © esdeem/
Shutterstock.com, 15; © belizar/Shutterstock.com, 18© Andrey_Kuzmin/Shutterstock.com, back cover

Library of Congress Cataloging-in-Publication Data

Calhoun, Kelly, author.
  Sneaky snouts / Kelly Calhoun.
  pages cm. — (Guess what)
  Summary: "Young children are natural problem solvers and always looking for answers, especially when it involves
animals. Guess What: Sneaky Snouts: Giant Anteater provides young curious readers with striking visual clues and
simply written hints. Using the photos and text, readers rely on visual literacy skills, reading, and reasoning as they
solve the animal mystery. Clearly written facts give readers a deeper understanding of how the animal lives. Additional
text features, including a glossary and an index, help students locate information and learn new words."
— Provided by publisher.
  Audience: Ages 5-8.
  Audience: K to grade 3.
  ISBN 978-1-63362-620-1 (hardcover) — ISBN 978-1-63362-710-9 (pbk.) — ISBN 978-1-63362-800-7 (pdf)
— ISBN 978-1-63362-890-8 (ebook)
  1. Myrmecophaga—Juvenile literature. [1. Anteaters.] I. Title.

QL737.E24C35 2016
599.3'14—dc23

2015003526

Cherry Lake Publishing would like to acknowledge the work of The Partnership for 21st Century Skills.
Please visit *www.p21.org* for more information.

Printed in the United States of America
Corporate Graphics Inc.

Table of Contents

My small eyes don't see very well.

I have long, sharp claws.

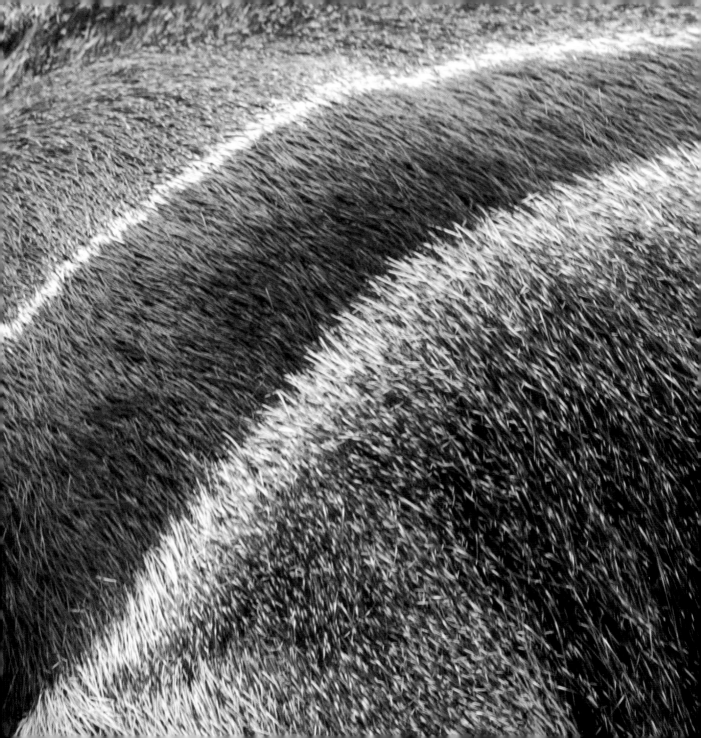

My body is covered with hair.

I have a long **nose** and a great sense of smell.

My ears are small and furry.

I have a long, sticky tongue.

I have a strong, bushy tail.

As a pup I rode on my mom's back.

Do you know what I am?

I'm a Giant Anteater!

About Giant Anteaters

1. Anteaters don't have teeth.

2. Pups are covered in fur at birth.

3. Anteaters' tongues are long and sticky.

4. Anteaters have long claws.

5. Giant anteaters can stand up on their hind legs.

Glossary

bushy (BUSH-ee) thick and spreading

sense (sens) one of the powers a living being uses to learn about its surroundings

sticky (STIK-ee) tending to stick to things when touched

Index